My Good Grief
Healing from Loss

Cheryl Parker

Healing is Rediscovering the Beauty of Life

Printed in the United States of America

First Printing, 2017

ISBN 13: 978-1544783819

ISBN 10:1544783817

Publisher: Create Space

Editor: Rebecca Camarena, Book Coach

Cover and Interior Design: Intention Media

Dedication

I dedicate this book to all those who have walked this healing journey before us and to all those who will follow behind us. But mostly, I dedicate this to YOU who has the courage to do this work and take this journey.

And also, to Shawn who has taken this walk of life with me. I love you dearly with heart wide open xo

Table of Contents

Acknowledgements

I believe we all have a purpose. I am also clear that not everyone will choose to explore or pursue their purpose and it is all okay whether you do or you don't. Growing up, I always longed to fit in and belong in order to feel normal, whatever my version of normal is and was. I grew up in a traditional environment. My immediate and extended family seemed to me, in hindsight, to play it safe. There were simple linear ways of thinking and acting: go to school, get good grades, behave, be polite, follow the rules, dinner at five, come home when the street lights come on and keep your nose clean. As we grew it became: get a job, work hard, buy a house, cut the grass, put the garbage out, be a good neighbour, shovel the driveway, pay your taxes, make yourself useful, volunteer to give back to your community. These rules of life kept me grounded and on track, yet all the while I was feeling like an alien, an odd ball, the black sheep, the weird one and never feeling like I fit in.

There was always a restlessness inside me, ants in my pants with a desire to break out of the traditional mould, break the dysfunctional cycle, follow my heart. It took a long time to finally embrace my differences to my traditional upbringing and throw away my perception of what was normal and start being okay with who I am: someone who wants to live a purpose driven life, change the world, is an ambassador of change and makes a mark, influences things that matter, leaves a legacy, allows myself to be a dreamer and is okay with ALL of who I am.

This workbook is an expression of me embracing who I am. I want to transform the conversation around loss. I experienced what I consider, many losses in my life and I did not have the language or the education and understanding from society in order to express it. I was never free to be real. I had an unshakeable determination and the courage to constantly tackle my unresolved issues and have sought out healing from every corner I could find. I am so grateful for all the people that were put in my path and were available to help me on this journey.

I acknowledge all the traditional people in my life that showed me my differences and that fuelled my drive and purpose, the mentors, teachers and healers I encountered along the way that empowered, encouraged, inspired and nurtured my healing. If I started shouting out names, I would inevitably forget someone. You know who you are. I am so fortunate to have you be a part of my journey. I love you eternally. All the clients I have worked with, it has been my privilege to work with you. Although I am the facilitator, I often come away feeling like the student because I learn so much about myself and the world through our workshops and sessions.

What people are saying about "My Good Grief"

"Before I took the My Good Grief Program, I was disconnected from myself, scared of men and the potential to open my heart, scared of being with people, scared of being abandoned, never following my heart, always wondering "What should I say?", "What should I do?", always comparing myself to others, always running, running, running with no purpose. After I took the My Good Grief Program with Cheryl in 2012, I dropped down into my heart and got access to being in the moment. I could be with myself, feel, express, stand for something, I was in touch with my desires, I had connection with myself and my loved ones who were here and loved ones that had died. I had forgiveness, peace of mind, I had direction and was in touch with my intuition and knowing, and could be generous with others because I was at peace with me."
J.G. 36, Female, Ghost Writer

"Before taking My Good Grief, life was complicated. I had a lot of anger, anxiety, unhappiness and high expectations of others. There was little relaxation or enjoyment of life and it was a chore to plan to go to events or outings as it was simply too much trouble and the ongoing stress created a lot of physical pain and exhaustion. I wanted to understand how to let go of the baggage that had been weighing me down for years, learn how to be less judgmental of others and learn how to let go of my need for everything to be perfect on the outside so people would not suspect what was going on inside and live a happier more rewarding life. I am now more relaxed, less critical of everyone else, kinder and gentler, but most importantly I am at peace with myself and where I am in

my life at this point in time. Having let go of stuff has opened up room for new experiences and I am having a lot of fun and success in my day-to-day activities now."
G.T. 65, Female, Online Sales Distributor

"My life had sunken into a terrible abyss, before I took the My Good Grief Program. My Father had passed away in September, a buddy of mine took his own life in November and a prominent lacrosse family lost their 8-year-old son to Cancer in December. I was finding it difficult to concentrate, days passed that I have no recollection of. My boss sat me down and told me that I needed to start putting the company first. What a kick in the teeth that was. My life seemed to be slowly spiraling out of control. I wanted to figure out how I could possibly get out from underneath the constant fog that had become my new reality. With Cheryl's expertise, I was able to navigate my way through the "My Good Grief" program. I was able to uncover the fact that the issue that I was grieving the most about, was not what brought me to the course. Over the course of eight weeks, I was able to work through my grief rather than masking or somehow sedating it. In short, I was given my life back and I began living again rather than existing. For this reason, I will be eternally grateful to Cheryl for her steadfast guidance and reassurance."
J.P. 52, Male, Market Specialist

"Thank you Cheryl! Teaching people how to deal with loss is so important. Before I took your course, I did not know how to effectively deal with the loss of my health. I felt like I was failing at life. I was unable to care for my daughter and me, the way I wanted to. Now I have skills and the way I see myself is completely different. Loss is a part of life and I do not judge myself any more. I did the best that I could do. I am

grateful for my illness it made me the person I am today. You are amazing I know you will continue to help a lot of people."
B.C. 47, Female, Entrepreneur

"I was struggling with grief and depression. I hoped to develop a better understanding of myself and how I interacted with those around me. The insight provided by the My Good Grief program has given me a deeper sense of self-awareness and balance throughout my daily life."
C.L. 23, Male, Student

"During an eighteen-month period of my life, I lost eight people that were close to me. My brother suddenly died after a few years of being ill from a hidden condition, a friend was killed in a car accident leaving his visitation, a few months later my aunt, and then my wonderful father… It was a steady stream of loss. Everyone felt like a blow to the stomach, and every time I pushed down the sadness, hoping the assault would stop. I was in pain, but denying it. Bouts of deep sadness and unexpected grief made me feel like I was out of control. I had a sense that I would be blindsided again at any moment, and for the first time in my life I became very anxious. I felt like I wasn't coping well, and I couldn't figure out how to change that. But I wanted it to be very different. After all, everyone loses someone close to them at some point, and they all seem to manage their loss. Why couldn't I? When I tried to talk to friends, most of them would freeze up, and I could tell it was a subject that wasn't welcome over a cup of coffee. But I wanted to learn how to grieve, because I felt like I didn't know what to do with everything I was feeling, and I definitely wanted to move past it. I wanted to feel like I did before losing so many people I love. I was so relieved to find My Good Grief. To be able to talk openly and freely in a very safe space, and to go through the process with Cheryl

was confronting, and at the same time life changing. I hear that phrase used a lot, but I truly did shift my views and experience, and that is life changing! Others talk about finding peace, but I didn't understand the depth of that word until I experienced it through this work. Peace, healing, and the ability to use what I've learned moving forward."
A.G. 56, Female, Co-founder of TotallyADD

"Cheryl helped me at a very hard time, that being the sudden loss of my son. She met with me shortly after his passing. I knew there was a rough road ahead, and I also knew I would need help right away to cope. Thankfully, the universe had Cheryl come into my life through a mutual friend. Each session we had helped me cope better every day. The exercises she had me complete from her workbook had such great impact during my loss, but also with past loss. She is a beautiful, wonderful soul and person who I cannot recommend enough to anyone who has dealt with loss and needs a loving guide to healing."
R.C. 45, Male, Actor

Introduction

Welcome to your journey of healing. This will be a very powerful pathway for you to get complete with the pain of your loss and heal your heart.

You probably have the experience of being broken hearted, and that's ok. When you experience a loss, that's a normal feeling. Of course you are going to feel like your heart is broken because you loved the person you lost whether it is a loss due to a broken relationship or a death. You could also be broken hearted due to a loss of trust, or loss of job, loss of financial status, loss of health or any number of other losses. The good news is, it is impossible for your heart to actually be broken. It feels like that, but that's not real, however, healing is.

There is good news and bad news in this. The good news is that you loved. The bad news is, the deeper you loved the more it will hurt. That's okay too. The ultimate good news is, that there is healing and it is right at your fingertips. That is why you have this workbook in your hands. You have already made a choice to heal at some level by virtue that we are connecting in this dialogue together.

Congratulations for making that choice and it is my honour to be guiding you through this path you are about to take. Fasten your seatbelt. It will sometimes be a rocky road but it's not dangerous, and it won't kill you or even harm you in any way, but there may be bumps along the way and curves on the path you weren't expecting and that's okay. Just stick with it. There is healing and joy at the end of the path.

Everyone learns in different ways. I am an experiential and visual learner so I have written this book in that way, because it's how I express myself. Some learn by listening, some by reading. My hope is that this workbook can speak to you, in a way for you to learn and get what you need, to heal your broken heart.

Pathways to Empowerment

Picture yourself walking on a path through the woods. It's sunny and the trees are beautiful with their leaves changing to their multi-coloured fall palettes. The ground is marked out where to walk, where many others have walked before you. The path is winding so you can't necessarily see where exactly you are going, but you can tell it leads to somewhere you haven't seen before. As you meander through the path, you might come across rocks you need to step over, and branches that have fallen on your pathway. Things might crunch uncomfortably under your feet that you weren't expecting, there might even be a few logs that have fallen across the path that make it appear that you won't be able to continue. At those times, I want you to picture yourself in those woods with that big log in your way. Look back over your shoulder and consider where you are on the path and take note that you've come this far, and to go back is the same distance behind you as there is ahead of you. And to go back the same distance will have you back where you started. And besides, there was a reason you started on this pathway to begin with, right? So you might as well climb over that log and get where you want to go.

You know that log is not a bigger challenge then you can handle...not really. It might look big and you might be tired from all the walking and not feel like climbing over it and your feet might be sore from the walking and this log is the perfect excuse to call it quits, but the log is definitely not bigger than you can handle. And you know it. You can soak those tired feet later and you can rest later and as I've pointed out, it's the same distance back as it is to go forward, but forward the rewards are plentiful, so just keep going. Nelson Mandela said "It seems impossible, until it is done."

The unknown is a strange phenomenon. We, as human beings tend to fear the unknown. If you think about fear – like someone has a loaded gun to your head kind of fear – that is REAL FEAR and the rest of the fear is actually made up in our heads of "what ifs" and "how abouts" and "ya, buts". Most of the time we fear things that never happen, thinking about it becomes our distraction and reason or excuse for not taking action in our lives. It's quite funny if you think about it (but don't think too long or it's another distraction ☺).

All that to say is, we can create many reasons to not take actions (or take pathways through the woods) when we don't know the way and don't know where we are going or where we will end up and that's not a good enough reason to not take the path.

If you have made it this far then I trust you are ready and willing to take the journey. If you are stopped along the way, come back to this section, read this analogy and get yourself back on the path.

Before We Head into the Woods

Picture yourself just on the fringe of a huge wooded area. It could be a field beside the woods or a gravel road beside the woods, or just a clearing in the woods beside a path leading into the denser part of the woods. There are two big tree stumps sticking two feet out of the ground side by side. Picture yourself taking a seat on one of these tree stumps and me on the other. Before we enter the woods and take this pathway we want to just sit and learn some things before we take our journey.

You might want to know some things about this guide that is about to take you through the woods on this pathway. Does she actually know the woods? Is she familiar with the path? Has she travelled on the path? Does she know how it winds? Will she know how to get me to the end? Will she be effective in guiding me over those logs?

Let me tell you with certainty I have taken this pathway many times and I have in the past both hated and loved this pathway, but in the end, have learned to only love it and I'm confident you will too. The reason for hating it is because I had to experience loss and who wants to do that?!?! Not me!

What I didn't know is that all through my life I was experiencing loss and just didn't know it. I didn't have the language for it, I didn't have the point of reference for it, and I certainly didn't have the tools or society's understanding and support for it. Not knowing I had been experiencing it all my life, it actually took the death of my eight year old daughter Rachel for me to sit up and take notice of what Grief was.

Let me just take a moment to tell you what happened to Rachel because it is my experience that when you say something like my eight year old daughter Rachel died, people tune out and are no longer listening. They are left distracted with a concern of "What happened to Rachel?" and are no longer in the conversation with me, so let's just address that first.

Rachel was a healthy little girl. A flu bug plagued our home in November 1998. First, my six year old Shawn got the flu, then me, and then Rachel. After a week, Rachel wasn't beating this virus and her stomach got hard. My mom and I took her to the local hospital Monday evening where they did an ultrasound and several tests and kept her in overnight for observation. In the morning, the paediatrician told me she had a condition called Idiopathic Thrombocytopenia Purpura (ITP). This means your antibodies attack your platelets instead of the virus. It is a 99% recoverable condition except Rachel was in the 1% where your antibodies get too low and can set off a spontaneous bleed, although that can be recoverable as well. Rachel was rushed to Sick Kid's Hospital in Toronto where they monitored her blood count and watched for spontaneous bleeding. There were no symptoms of this until ten o'clock Tuesday evening when her eyes glossed over and she became agitated after having been lethargic for two days. She couldn't move her left side and I could see behind her glossy eyes her cries for help. The medical staff came running and a CT Scan confirmed she had a spontaneous bleed in her brain. They started pumping her with platelets to prepare her for surgery while her antibodies continued to attack them. Once the platelets were at a high enough level that she wouldn't bleed to death, they performed brain surgery to remove the front left lobe of her brain to release the pressure. After a couple of hours of surgery, they knew, her brain was too swollen and they couldn't save her. She was pronounced brain dead. Monday she had the flu, Tuesday she was in brain surgery and Wednesday she was dead.

The death of my daughter brought me to my knees – like it would.

This is when I really learned what Grief was. I have continued to learn so much over the years about Grief from my own experiences and the experiences from those I have coached.

Let's start with the definitions of Grief vs. Mourning

Mourning is different than Grieving.

Mourning is the physical actions or expressions of one who has experienced a loss. Examples of this are crying, yelling, wearing black, etc.

Grieving is the emotional, deep mental anguish experienced by someone who has had a loss. Examples of this are deep sorrow, feelings of a heavy heart, forgetfulness, lack of concentration etc.

❖ ❖ ❖ ❖ ❖ ❖ ❖ ❖ ❖ ❖ ❖ ❖ ❖ ❖ ❖

Once I had experienced this catastrophic loss – from which I decided from the "get go" that I would never recover – what I didn't count on, was all the other losses boiling up to the surface. Healing wasn't going to happen easily unless I acknowledged ALL OF IT. That was so strange to me. For me, the way my brain operates is, I compartmentalize things: this "is this" and that "is that". But not so, in my healing journey.

The losses collided and I was not counting on that at all. And it wasn't like I was even consciously aware of this. It's only in hindsight that I can even explain it to you. It all revealed itself in an ugly messy way. Like falling apart emotionally with no explanation when I thought I was doing really well, coping with it all, then hitting my bottom and reaching out for help.

I was attending a healing circle with a group of women I knew from my community and we were all sharing what our dreams were. People were sharing anything from a new house, to a trip they always wanted, to mending a relationship, etc. All I could think about was wanting to hug Rachel one more time. My dream seemed so simple compared to everyone else, but mine was the most unattainable and I fell apart. I started crying uncontrollably, became non-responsive, my limbs became weak and all I could do was sit and stare into space. I was there but not there.

I just wanted to leave the earth, leave my body and float away. I figured I had lost my mind, but yet I was aware of everyone around me, people asking me questions and my knowing the answers but not wanting to speak. I just wanted to die. I knew they all wanted to help, but I actually didn't want their help. I just wanted them to leave me alone. I answered some questions in a spacey, ultra calm way, but all I wanted to do was float away. Funny, it is only in writing now that I remember this, I had forgotten about this incident. It really was a turning point for me.

That's when everything bubbled up into one pot of grief that had to be acknowledged and embraced in its entirety, then healed from.

There is no such thing as compartmentalizing the grief (what I thought I was doing at the time). And there is no way to go around it, under it or over it. You must go *through it* to get to the other side. Taking a helicopter ride over the woods and looking down on the path does not equal walking the path. And looking at someone's pictures of their walk through the woods is not the same as walking it yourself. And looking into the woods from the tree stump we are sitting on, does not mean you know the path. It is only in strapping on that backpack of *pathway lessons* and taking the trek yourself that you **REALLY GO THROUGH THE PATHWAY.**

Pathway Lesson #2

When you have a BIG LOSS in your life, it is inevitable that all the other incomplete losses will boil up to the surface.

*Let me define **Big Loss**. It is a loss that, <u>for you</u> is considered BIG. It is subjective and unique for everyone. What is experienced as a Big Loss for one person, may not be as big to another, depending on your life experiences and relationship to the loss. You say what is a Big and Small Loss in your life. All losses have different intensities to all of us.*

❖ ❖ ❖ ❖ ❖ ❖ ❖ ❖ ❖ ❖ ❖ ❖ ❖ ❖ ❖

You can't go over it, around it, or under it, you must go through it.

There are no short cuts in this process, you must go into every corner and discover what you didn't know, or see before, in order to get complete. Otherwise, it isn't complete. (And COMPLETE is the perfect word to describe it!)

❖　❖　❖　❖　❖　❖　❖　❖　❖　❖　❖　❖　❖　❖　❖

My mission is to equip everyone with the tools so they can deal with each and every one of their losses. I am not saying I can prevent people from feeling despair of any loss. I am though saying I can soften the blow and reduce the suffering by educating people so it doesn't have to be a situation where you have to deal with ALL OF IT in one fell swoop.

I can't imagine that if I knew then what I know now I wouldn't have still experienced total despair over the loss of my daughter. But in hindsight, I can see how I could have recovered quicker and more simply if I knew what I know now. And please don't misunderstand me. The process is the process and that was my process and I would not change any of it – REALLY!! There was nothing wrong with the way I did my recovery and there is nothing wrong with the way you are doing your recovery. The bottom line is, that there is no right or wrong way to grieve, there is just the way <u>YOU</u> grieve.

It follows then that I have to confront that this workbook is not the right way to do your grieving and nor is it the wrong way. Of course, I want this workbook to be the "be all and end all" for you, but I have read so many books, seen so many healers, attended so many workshops, watched so many

16

videos, etc. etc. etc. The list is huge with what I took on to heal myself and I wouldn't discount any of it.

Pathway Lesson #4

There is no right or wrong way to grieve. There is just the way you grieve.

Like I mentioned earlier, just as everyone learns differently, everyone reacts differently to circumstances and life events. I could write a whole book on this topic. Personalities, past and present life experiences, and so much more all contribute to how people grieve. Giving yourself permission to grieve the way you grieve, is a gift to yourself. Give yourself this gift.

❖ ❖ ❖ ❖ ❖ ❖ ❖ ❖ ❖ ❖ ❖ ❖ ❖ ❖ ❖

When Rachel died I was surrounded by support from neighbours, co-workers, friends, family and acquaintances from the community. Everyone was well meaning and yet there is an inherited conversation around grief that in my opinion, doesn't work. It seems to me that people are very awkward around the conversation of grief and therefore end up saying things just for the sake of saying something. Society is conditioned to "look on the bright side" which totally avoids dealing with grief (remember Pathway Lesson #3 - no short cuts!). People who have not had to deal with the loss you are experiencing are too afraid they might have to feel it someday and who wants to go there...nobody!!! People don't want to see people they care about go through it either. None of us enjoy seeing anyone in pain, so we want to immediately "cheer them up" or avoid making them "feel bad", however, all that does is stop the feeling or delay it or make the person grieving feel that they are not "doing it right".

Examples of this for me were, "don't feel bad, Rachel is in a better place" or "at least you still have Shawn", or "you can have other children", or my favourite (not!) "perhaps there was a Paul Bernardo in her future and God took her to avoid that fate" (oh great, now I have two fates to consider for my daughter: either my daughter being savagely sexually tortured and living, or dying). I guess I should be happy and grateful she is dead and I should thank God for protecting her from the uglier fate she was doomed for. Does any of this seem ridiculous to you? I promise you, these are real things people said to me when Rachel died. People loved me with all their heart and just did not want me to feel bad. But here's a news flash: my daughter died. I'm supposed to feel bad. They just didn't want to feel bad and didn't want me to either.

There are so many cliché's are used in different scenarios. For example with divorce or end of friendship or romantic relationship: "you're better off without them," "you'll find someone else that you deserve," "there are other fish in the sea." For miscarriages: "you can have other children," "it wasn't meant to be," "at least you know you can get pregnant." For pets: "you can get another dog," "they have a short life span." For health, injury and accidents: "you're lucky to be alive," "it could have been worse."

Another classic for me was shortly after Rachel died, I was in the elevator with someone I knew from work and they didn't speak to me. It was as if I wasn't there. It was weird. I had known this person for years. They just stood with their head down and then got off the elevator. They told me later they wanted to say how sorry they were that my daughter had died but didn't want to remind me and bring me down in case I was having a good day. Think about that for a minute. Do you think that at any moment over the years I have ever forgotten that my daughter died? Do you honestly think that by acknowledging her death it is going to bring me down if I am having a good day? It's hilarious, right? This was a normal reaction I ran into many times. These were people who knew me for twenty years and cared about me or they wouldn't have been trying to be careful around me. But people just don't know what to say or how to react to someone in pain. We just are not taught how to be with this conversation. It's nobody's fault, we are just taught what our parents were taught and so on. It just keeps getting handed down the generations.

This inherited conversation around grief leaves the griever isolated and also the people around them that really want to support the griever, isolated as well. We are paralyzed with no words or the words that just come out to say "something" but don't actually support the person we care about when we really would like nothing more than to help or support or let them know we care.

There is something fundamentally "off" with this inherited conversation about grief. This is an area I am committed to transforming. I want us all to be able to talk about grief like it is a normal conversation like talking about the weather. Everyone deals with weather and it's not a big deal to discuss it whether it's good or bad. Everyone deals with loss so why not talk about that, like it is a normal topic?

By stuffing down what is really on our hearts, we are cutting ourselves off from the love we could be sharing with another human being, we are denying ourselves healing and connection with others. I say, if you REALLY don't know what to say. Say exactly that, "I really don't know what to say". Sometimes people said that and I totally agreed with their sentiments because sometimes, I didn't either. That was sometimes the most honest and comforting thing people said.

Don't use cliché's to comfort a loved one.

In these awkward situations, we fumble for the right thing to say, and we want to look on the bright side and we want to say something to make them feel better, but the truth is, they are going through a life experience, they are supposed to feel lousy in these situations, it would not be authentic for them to be any other way than the way they are feeling, so speaking in cliché's really does nothing to comfort them. They will smile politely, but it could do more harm than good. We don't know how those comments could be perceived and it is my experience from people that they usually offend them more than comfort them. These cliché's sometimes may be true, but let the griever grieve first. They will find their way to these answers as they heal. Skipping over the sadness onto brighter skies just delays the process. Stay away from the cliché's when your loved one is first going through the circumstance that causes them grief.

❖ ❖ ❖ ❖ ❖ ❖ ❖ ❖ ❖ ❖ ❖ ❖ ❖ ❖ ❖

If you don't know what to say, just say exactly that, "I don't know what to say." It's honest and true. Speak from the heart.

We know this to be true generally, we just need to apply this when we are faced with difficult situations. It's all you would want isn't it? for people to just speak to you from their heart. We can't undo what has been done and all we really want to do is comfort the ones in pain. Speak from the heart.

❖ ❖ ❖ ❖ ❖ ❖ ❖ ❖ ❖ ❖ ❖ ❖ ❖ ❖ ❖

I remember wanting to get through the grieving as quickly as possible so I could get back to life and feel normal again. Rachel died on December 2nd and her organs were harvested on December 3rd. The visitation at the funeral home was December 4th and her funeral was December 5th. I remember being in a robotic state and thinking very calmly and clearly about what had to be done logistically in my life. There were Christmas presents to be bought, forms to fill in for short term disability, people were booking me for coffee dates and lunch dates, so there was a schedule to fulfill while I was off work. My parents wouldn't allow me to drive so there were driving arrangements to be made, social workers from the kid's school to speak to, a trust fund to manage, newspaper and television interviews to coordinate, Shawn's activities to manage and so on. In my mind I was very busy taking care of business so that after Christmas, I could get Shawn settled back into school and I could return to work and we could start putting the pieces of our lives back together. I was after all, a very successful, independent, capable, and driven individual. That was just my personality. That was just a perfectly natural way for me to be operating.

Christmas came and went and I know I went through the motions because there are pictures, but I have no recollection of the event even to this day. After New Year's, Shawn returned to school and was welcomed by his classmates who had come by for visits, made him cards and given him gifts. I returned to work and was greeted by "What are you doing here?" "Are you crazy?" and "Go home!" OKAY, I wasn't exactly sharp, but I needed to get back to something normal. I wanted my life to go back somehow to the way it used to be. And no matter how much I forced it, I kept getting pushed back.

Pathway Lesson #7

Keeping busy is a coping skill to deal with Grief.

❖   ❖   ❖   ❖   ❖   ❖   ❖   ❖   ❖   ❖   ❖   ❖   ❖   ❖   ❖

I started doing what people told me I should do. Go see this counsellor, go read this book, attend this seminar, and go to this support group. I did it all in robotic fashion, judging and assessing everyone else but not seeing where I was at. I hated all the people at the support group, they were all wallowing in their grief several years after their loss. They seemed to be in worse shape than me and I was determined I wasn't going to be where they were three years from then. No way! Not me! I'm going to get through this in record time. I'm Cheryl Parker!

I despised the women from the other support group who seemed uncaring with comments like "If I see another lasagne I will throw it at my neighbour." I thought, how ungrateful can you be? Another woman asked me if I had done any cooking yet? And I said, "yes, every night, why?" They thought that

22

was heroic because they had been living on take-out. I thought, "What is wrong with these people? Snap out of it. I have a son to feed, so of course I cook for goodness sake!" Those support groups did not work out so well for me. Onwards and upwards. At least I tried it right? ☺

I can now see how judgemental I was about them in my comparing everyone and wanting to be "better" than everyone else in this situation (and making sure they all knew it). I was going to breeze through this faster than everyone else too. I had to forgive myself and again, it would have gone very differently if I knew what I know now, but this was all part of my learning, growing and healing.

Pathway Lesson #8

Keeping our judgements about how others grieve will keep us from grieving ourselves.

❖ ❖ ❖ ❖ ❖ ❖ ❖ ❖ ❖ ❖ ❖ ❖ ❖ ❖ ❖ ❖

I would seek healing in every place I could think of. I attended a local church that I had grown up in and I decided I would be the new Superintendent of the Sunday school and minister to the children of the community. This would be a way to connect with the children and fill the void. So I took that on, and raised the attendance to more than four times the number of kids than were attending before. People referred to me as "an inspiration" and "a pillar of strength for our community."

I became the National Spokesperson for Organ Donation and was participating in television and radio interviews, working on documentaries and was flown to Winnipeg to appear on a panel for organ donation on Women's Television Network. I was also doing a lot of public speaking events as a motivational speaker.

Pathway Lesson #9

Seeking accolades for how you grieve can be a coping skill.

I think we look for reassurance that we are doing okay ourselves because we don't always know which way is up when we are in the throes of grief. So it would be very common (if this is your personality or a common way for you to cope) to take on things to seek accolades. This is not a bad thing, any more than any of our other coping skills. They are good things to have. It is only when they prevent you from healing that these activities become a problem that you need to perhaps step back and assess.

❖   ❖   ❖   ❖   ❖   ❖   ❖   ❖   ❖   ❖   ❖   ❖   ❖   ❖   ❖

I was spending a lot of my time off making sure everyone knew I was okay. And I was making sure they were okay and helping them deal with the loss. I didn't want anyone to be suffering over me. I would meet friends for lunch and talk to them about how they were, keep in touch with Rachel's and Shawn's friends and make sure they were all okay.

Pathway Lesson #10

Taking care of others or being strong for others can be a coping skill.

This can be true for both men and women. Although genders can grieve differently, I see a parallel with this lesson. Women are the nurturers and want to take care of everyone and can be selfless in these situations. On the other hand, men are

24

taught to be "the head of the household," or "the man of the house." A man would feel a lot of pressure to make sure everyone else is okay at the expense of his own healing. I see this also the case of the oldest siblings wanting to be there for younger siblings, or caregivers to elderly or unhealthy friends, family, parents with adult children that are grieving. Not to mention the pressures on all grievers from society to "be strong" and for them to let everyone think they are "okay" and "doing well." This is a common one. Watch out for this one.

❖ ❖ ❖ ❖ ❖ ❖ ❖ ❖ ❖ ❖ ❖ ❖ ❖ ❖ ❖

I have shared some of the insights I have learned from my own grieving process and those of others I have coached. I have given you real examples in these stories but, you need to find yourself in these stories and relate them to your situation and your grief and your way of coping. If you need to go back and read the lessons again, then do so, this is about you. Remember, no right way. There is no rule that you have to have it all figured out after reading through once. It is easy for our minds to wander. Do what you need to do to get the most out of this workbook. This is your healing journey and very well worth the time and effort you will put into it.

Now comes the experiential part of the learning. Putting pen to paper is an essential part of this program. It's one thing to think about it and "know" the answer, but writing it down has a purpose. Something gets transferred from internal to external. You have enough internal you are dealing with. Let's get it out onto paper. Don't skip this part. Remember "Trust the Process." I will call these REST STOPS.

REST STOP

What is the definition of mourning?

_____

What is the definition of grieving?

_____

How do you know whether you are grieving or depressed? Ultimately you need to see a professional for a diagnosis, but how I knew for myself that I was grieving is that I did not lose my sense of humour. I had a will inside to move forward even though I felt like I was fighting something deep inside me that was telling me otherwise.

What are some of the mourning signs you are experiencing?

_____

_____

What are some of the grieving signs you are experiencing?

_____

_____

What cliché's have people said to you and how did you react?

_____

_____

_____

What coping skills have you used to cope with Grief?

_____

_____

_____

_____

During the first year of my healing, I took a trip to Hawaii with a really close friend and I remember being in a store admiring a sweater but it was more expensive then I was used to paying for a sweater. My friend said "Tell me you're not going to squabble over the price of that sweater. If it makes you happy, buy it". I decided buying nice things for myself could make me happy. And my external habit was born. I would shop to make me happy and so I shopped, and shopped, and shopped. And it did work, but it was always a short term fix. So I had to shop more to keep the feeling going. We will explore this experience a bit deeper on our journey together through this book.

Pathway Lesson #11

It is common to use external habits to distract you from having to feel the pain you are experiencing. Things such as alcohol, drugs, shopping, movies, excessive exercise, over working, over eating, internet, television, smoking are all distractions

❖ ❖ ❖ ❖ ❖ ❖ ❖ ❖ ❖ ❖ ❖ ❖ ❖ ❖ ❖

I was driving with Shawn and couldn't remember where we were going. I pulled off to the side of the road and started crying. Shawn asked, "what's wrong mommy?" I in turn asked him, "where are we going?" and he replied "to get me a hair cut." I had to take a look around me and get my bearings of what road we were on, and how to navigate myself to where Shawn gets his hair cut. I could picture the plaza where we were going, but couldn't automatically figure out how to get there. It took a few minutes to sort it out in my mind and then I was good to go, and started driving again and thanked Shawn and assured him I knew where we were going now and how to get there.

Pathway Lesson #12

Some of the symptoms people experience when they are grieving are lack of concentration, lack of motivation, forgetfulness, exhaustion, physical body pain, trouble following instructions, inability to retain information, anxiety and stress.

❖ ❖ ❖ ❖ ❖ ❖ ❖ ❖ ❖ ❖ ❖ ❖ ❖ ❖ ❖

When I was driving away from the hospital when Rachel was pronounced brain dead, I remember being in the back seat of my parents' van and looking out the window. Everything looked grey. The sky was grey, the buildings in Toronto were all grey, everyone was wearing grey. It was all grey. I remember thinking, my world just lost all of its colour. I might survive this, but I will never let this be ok. It will never be okay that Rachel died and I will never feel joy in my heart. I had just written myself a life sentence of misery.

Pathway Lesson #13

We are making decisions all the time. When we make these declarations we create our inevitable future. Thoughts can and do come true.

The good news about this is that we made them up and we can make up new ones. I rewrote my whole story and I always have joy in my heart and its okay that Rachel died.

❖ ❖ ❖ ❖ ❖ ❖ ❖ ❖ ❖ ❖ ❖ ❖ ❖ ❖ ❖

What are some of your external habits/distractions?

_____

_____

_____

_____

_____

_____

What are some of your symptoms?

_____

_____

_____

_____

_____

_____

_____

What are some of the decisions you have made that have played out in your life?

_____

_____

_____

_____

_____

As you are probably seeing by now, there are many lessons to learn before heading into the woods. All these lessons let you know who you are with regards to grief. And I can tell you no two people are the same. We all learn different conversations passed on through our families from generation to generation. And then we have our own circumstances and our own personality thrown into the mix and voila, there you are.

It is always a natural thing to make ourselves wrong for how we cope or our symptoms, or our distractions, but they are all there to serve us. They are not wrong. It is also natural to make others wrong for teaching you this information or passing on their advice or the things they said to you in times of need. They are not wrong either. We all do the best we can with the knowledge we have and we are only thinking we are generous by passing our teachings onto others. It doesn't help anyone by making them wrong about doing or sharing it.

The only way we can make a difference is to make it all okay. You are okay and others are ok. Everyone will grieve differently depending on their inherited conversations and their circumstances and personalities.

So let's agree to just let that all be okay just the way it is and just the way it isn't. It's really the only way you can move forward to healing. If you can't let it be okay, then let's just put it aside for now at least and we can come back to it later.

With everything being okay, what can you now see for yourself? Can you see that there are symptoms that you are no longer willing to put up with? Are there symptoms that are sucking the aliveness out of your life? Are the symptoms stealing your happiness?

Are your coping skills only getting you so much success? Are your distractions keeping you from really healing? If you said yes to any of these then you are ready to venture into the woods.

You will need to pack all these lessons in your back pack before we go into the woods. We will need them all on our travels.

So now, there is the gear you wear. It really doesn't matter what brand name of hiking boots you wear or the type of jacket you wear as long as you have one. There are so many different name brands to choose from just like there are so many different losses you could be dealing with. Now we all know there are the obvious brands like Nike, New Balance, Merrell, North Face. It's the same for the hiking vests. One might automatically think about Marmot and North Face as the obvious choices, but as you know the list would be endless if you started really looking at them all. Once you take the time to sift through all the name brands you would see brands you hadn't even seen before, not to mention the different styles and colours. The list of shoes and vests would be lengthy. And everyone would choose a different one based on their taste and what fits them.

It's the same when you look at your losses. We often think about death as the only loss that gets any recognition. If you think about it, divorce is so common people don't seem to bat an eyelash when someone declares that they are leaving their husband or wife. Closer friends and family probably engage more in the circumstances around the situation but I believe regular interactions would be pretty brief. There are many different losses that people experience and no two losses are the same, and no two people would have the same list.

What is some of the gear you are wearing? List some of the losses you have experienced:

_____

_____

_____

_____

There may be some that you didn't even think were considered losses such as miscarriages, moving, changing schools, retirement, loss of health or mobility from illness or accident, loss of confidence, loss of trust, loss of protection, loss of stability, menopause, empty nest, loss of safety, loss of self, and sometimes it is the loss of an opportunity you thought you were going to have or the loss of dreams you once had. Whatever the loss (gear) you are wearing, it has left you feeling unfilled in life and that is what you are carrying around.

Loss can be a tricky thing. When looked at as an isolated incident, it can appear fairly harmless, and with the intelligence and knowledge you have, you can easily feel that it is "not a big deal". Society would have you put a positive slant on it, and think of others worse off, or to be grateful for what you have. That then leads you to dismiss the loss because for you to "dwell" on it would look like you are not coping with your life. So you carry on, accumulating losses, carrying each one and securing your coping strategies into place such that they become the normal way to instead of the exception when something happens that is unpleasant. Your habits are formed and it becomes the new normal.

What you are not aware of is the veil of discomfort and unfulfilled life expectations and experiences that have been

33

slowly sweeping over you and your senses. Then you wake up one day and you are unhappy and can't figure out why because for all intents and purposes, you have everything that a person could want; from the outside looking in, you have it made. So why are you unhappy? So yet again you carry on and ignore it because it is so easy to dismiss this in the big scheme of things. Society begs for us to look on the bright side and be grateful. And I'm not saying that is a bad thing to be grateful, it is a wonderful thing, it just can be deceiving and have us skip over the grief and miss the healing needed and wanted.

Journal your thoughts here:

_____

_____

_____

_____

_____

_____

_____

_____

_____

_____

_____

_____

_____

_____

_____

_____

_____

_____

_____

_____

Off to the Woods – Our Map

So the next step we need to take as we enter the woods on our path, is to draw a map. We will call this our My Good Grief Map.

Get a piece of paper and draw a map of the path. Make it as straight or winding as you wish, draw a map of your life with all the bends and turns that your life has taken with the losses you have experienced. Be as creative as you wish, or just draw a straight path with your losses. If you are taking the creative route, feel free to demonstrate where the hills and valleys are.

Here are some examples of loss for you to reference: death of a loved one (friend, family, pet, co-worker), moving, retirement, divorce, loss of health, loss of mobility, loss of trust, loss of self-esteem, loss of innocence through sexual abuse, loss of faith, empty nest, loss of safety from rape, crime or theft, loss of protection, loss of self, loss of home from fire or flood and on and on.

Once you complete your map. Take a moment to reflect on the map and journal some thoughts you have about the path your life has taken. There is no "right" way to feel. You might think wow I have had a lot of losses. I have handled my life well. Or you might think, wow now it makes sense why I am the way I am, based on all these experiences I have had or you might be sad revisiting all your losses. You might be surprised to see how many losses and realize you have never looked at your life in this way. You might remember losses you had forgotten about. You might realize there was a big loss earlier on in your life that is still affecting you now that you didn't realize. You might realize that there is a loss that is still affecting you that is not the one that brought you to consider taking this journey in the first place. Or you might think something completely different. Your responses are going to be as individual as your losses.

Take a moment and journal your thoughts here:

_____

_____

_____

_____

_____

_____

_____

_____

Now that we have our map, we need to use it for our walk. It's best to utilize the map on your journey. You wouldn't just check your map once and stick it in your backpack. You would refer to it along the way. So we will be using our map as we take our pathway.

Map Exercise #1

Have a look at your map and check for all your losses. Rate your losses from 1 – 4 with the following criteria. Just put the number beside the loss and circle it.

1 – Feels like it happened yesterday – very painful

2 – Can still feel the pain but it has subsided somewhat

3 – It just hurts when I think about it, but doesn't come to mind very often

4 – Haven't thought about it in forever, and even when I do, it's not painful

❖ ❖ ❖ ❖ ❖ ❖ ❖ ❖ ❖ ❖ ❖ ❖ ❖ ❖ ❖

Map Exercise #2

Remember the lessons we learned before we entered the woods? If you don't, take a peek back at your notes. Look at (i) Cliché's (ii) Symptoms (iii) Distractions and (iv) Decisions you recognized for yourself. Now map them onto your pathway of losses. This will allow you to see where the cliché's originated from. Not to make them wrong, but just to recognize when they were birthed into your life and the impact they may have had on you. Then you can see the symptoms you had associated with the loss and the distractions you used to cope and then the decisions you made when you experienced the different losses.

Start with your #1 losses and work down to the #4 losses. You may not necessarily have a cliché, symptom, distraction and decision for every loss, but fill in what you can. This will take some time so allow yourself 30 – 60 minutes to do this exercise. This is the work. You are in the dense part of the woods. By all means, look up and enjoy and take in the beauty of the trees, flowers, and wild life but then put your head down and walk the path.

❖ ❖ ❖ ❖ ❖ ❖ ❖ ❖ ❖ ❖ ❖ ❖ ❖ ❖ ❖

If it makes it easier, get a separate piece of paper and write them this way

Loss: Miscarriage

Cliché: You can try again, it's God's way of taking care of what is not perfect, and, at least you know you can get pregnant

Symptom: Sad, angry, didn't want to talk about it, felt alone, worried I would not be able to have children

Distraction: Pretend I didn't want kids, emotional eating, drinking

Decision: I'm not going to tell anyone if I get pregnant again, unless I am six months along and no chance of miscarrying

What do you notice in doing this exercise? There is no right answer. It is individual for everyone. This will fill in even more blanks for you as you see who you are as it relates to grief and how you got to be who you are.

REST STOP

Let's take a moment and celebrate who you are as it relates to grief.

What have you overcome?

_____

_____

_____

_____

What strengths have you gained from your losses?

_____

_____

_____

_____

What vulnerabilities have been exposed due to your grief experiences?

_____

_____

_____

_____

What are some of your personal triumphs?

_____

_____

_____

_____

Let's just reflect on that for a moment. We are extremely resilient when it comes to loss. It is inevitable that we will all deal with loss. But it is more important who we are in the face of loss. And it is not always easy.

Let's look at the impacts loss has had on your life.

What are the impacts you have had to deal with because of loss?

_____

_____

_____

_____

What have you missed out on because of loss?

_____

_____

_____

_____

How has loss impacted you financially?

_____

_____

_____

_____

What is the impact on your health and vitality due to loss?

_____

_____

_____

What other impacts can you think of?

_____

_____

_____

Loss is not without impacts as you can see once you pull it all apart and look at it in this way. It is my hope that in seeing all the impacts that an accumulation of loss can have in your life, will have you consider that this is not the way you want to feel any more. I can only assume that you already started thinking this way when you picked up this workbook, but this exercise will have you really see what the impacts are on you and also be able to celebrate how well you have coped up until now. This can also give you an appreciation for everyone around you in your life and how each person's situation is different and how we are all impacted differently and cope differently depending on how things play out in our lives. When you finish your journey through the workbook you will not only have more compassion and education for yourself but also have the compassion and education to assist others when they are experiencing loss.

One of the ways we can have compassion for ourselves (and others) is to honour the feelings that are there and not ignore, minimize or compare them to others. Having my loss be less than your loss gets none of us to the place of healing. If my daughter died and you are sad because your daughter is going away to university or moving across the country, should one mother feel worse than the other? Should one mother not have the right to feel sad? Should one mother hide her feelings because of what the other mother has experienced? Well, you could, but it doesn't get anyone to a place of peace. The mother whose daughter died is left isolated and unable to comfort her friend and the mother who's daughter is moving across the country cannot honour her own feelings. Nobody wins in this scenario. What would the world look like if we all had permission to express how we REALLY ARE? Free to be REAL. I believe there is a perception that you will be a "downer" if you are talking about something that is sad. I can assure you I am not someone that the people around me would consider to be a "downer" but I express what is REALLY going on and it brings humanness to conversation and nobody leaves the room crying. We leave the room more connected and alive to our senses. ☺

Map Secret #1

If you are unable to talk about the loss, chances are you are incomplete and there is healing in this next phase of the journey.

❖ ❖ ❖ ❖ ❖ ❖ ❖ ❖ ❖ ❖ ❖ ❖ ❖ ❖ ❖

Map Secret #2

If you want to find where you are incomplete, ask yourself, "what do I wish was different, better or more?"

❖ ❖ ❖ ❖ ❖ ❖ ❖ ❖ ❖ ❖ ❖ ❖ ❖ ❖ ❖

REST STOP

What would it be like for you if you could talk about your loss and not feel limited or constrained with the people in your life?

_____

_____

_____

_____

_____

_____

It is up to you to consider and decide whether you are incomplete or not and it is up to you to take responsibility for the loss remaining incomplete. The good news about that is once you declare it is incomplete and that you are responsible for having it remain incomplete, you are completely free to take the necessary steps in getting the loss complete.

Taking responsibility does not mean you are at fault for something. This is not to criticize you for a mistake or an inadequacy on your part. It is the ability to carry forward an action to ensure success. Said another way, if you break down the word R-E-S-P-O-N-S-I-B-I-L-I-T-Y. It could be broken down as the "ability" to "respond". You are the one that is incomplete and you have the _ability to respond_ to that. Besides, with loss, nobody else can get you complete. If you are not responsible for your own completeness, then you are looking for someone else to take an action for your peace of mind (which might never happen). So it is actually good news that you are responsible for your own completeness with your loss.

Log on the Path

As we walk through the forest, we come across a large tree that has fallen and we see the tree laying there in the forest, lifeless and all that is left behind is the huge hole in the ground with exposed soil and the destruction around it. There is no possible way of propping that tree back up in the hole and having it be as it once was.

There will be times during your healing when there are obstacles in your way of getting to where you want to be and no seemingly obvious way of restoring the damage.

Most times it is the conversations in our mind that are stopping us from continuing on the path (the log that has fallen in our way).

Sometimes we can't fathom life without this person no matter how we try. One of the common questions people ask or struggle with and don't necessarily even realize is, "Who am I without this person? pet? job? faith? or…" Fill in the blank.

I know for me, I did not know who I was without my daughter. Even though I was still a mother to my son Shawn, I was no longer the mother of Rachel & Shawn and that rocked my foundation. The hole just seemed too big. It seemed like I had to fill it, but there was nothing to fill it with. And so healing for me meant recreating myself as to who I was going to be. I love the quote "Life is not about finding yourself, it is about creating yourself." That is exactly what my experience was. When Rachel died I lost myself and found myself all in one.

When I chose to leave my eighteen year career, I didn't anticipate how much of my identity came from my career, and struggled with "who am I" if I'm not a corporate business woman.

When my friend's dog died, she struggled with who she was without her dog. Her whole routine came to an abrupt halt. No dog to greet in the morning, no dog to take for walk, no community to socialize with at the dog park, no dog to feed and care for. It is an abrupt interruption to what you know in your life and what gives you who you are.

You can be dealing with disorganization, confusion, searching, yearning, and feeling like you are crazy! It could feel like you have been dropped into a play with no script. It will help you to know that things have to get disorganized before it can be reorganized. Confusion and disorganization are stepping stones towards your healing.

Yearning and preoccupation with memories can be draining, as can difficulty with eating and sleeping. This could go either way, eating and sleeping too much or not eating and sleeping enough.

Anxiety, panic and fear are other experiences you may have. Another question you may be faced with is, "Will I survive this?" I remember being so surprised that I actually survived it when my daughter died. The "it" being the grief. I thought the Grief would take me out.

People have told me they have said things out loud that don't make sense and don't even know why they said it. Someone shared with me a situation where they saw an object that was clearly red, but said it was blue and didn't know why they said that.

I remember thinking that since Rachel's ultimate situation was a brain injury caused by complications from a flu bug, I was so connected to her, I must have brain damage as well.

It was explained to me at the time, that shock has a way of protecting our brains and it is a good thing. Taking on all that was reality at that time would be too much for the brain. That made sense to me and gave me comfort that my faculties would return through my healing.

The fear of what the future holds can be paralyzing. Your energy is drained and you can easily be overwhelmed. Fear of your financial status can also add to the crippling feelings. When I gave up my corporate career I worried about being able to support myself and my son.

You might be surprised at how physical the grieving process can be. Feelings of emptiness in your stomach, tightness in your throat, digestive problems, heart palpitations, etc. Your body will communicate the stress you are experiencing. Self-care is paramount during this time and yet you may not feel like taking care of yourself. That's when you need to allow people around you to care for you.

Explosive emotions can also show up unexpectedly. Any emotion such as sadness, anger, blame, resentment, and jealousy can all be magnified while you are grieving.

I remember driving up to the Port Office one day and seeing Rachel's friend with her Mom walking towards the building. I didn't want to get out of my car. I didn't feel up to facing anyone that day, never mind one of Rachel's buddies. I sat there in my car and this overwhelming sadness and rage came over me. I smashed my hand on the steering wheel and said "Why can't Rachel go to the Post Office with me today?" I kept hitting the steering wheel. I was so mad and felt so ripped off from life's simple tasks. I resented everyone that got to do the things that I should be able to do. I screamed and cried and yelled at God while sitting in the Post Office parking lot. Another moment when I thought I was losing my mind. I'm sure if anyone saw me that day they would have confirmed it ☺

REST STOP

What logs are on your path?

_____

_____

_____

_____

What do you have to say about your logs?

_____

_____

_____

Do you have any physical symptoms? If so, what are they?

_____

_____

_____

What are some of the ways you are allowing others to care for you?

_____

_____

_____

What are some ways you could or are taking care of yourself?

_____

_____

_____

_____

It is in these times, when we are faced with these logs on our path, that we are really in touch with who we are and what we are made of. Sometimes we are lucky to have loved ones around us to hold us up through the grieving process, but it really comes from inside. You have to go inside and touch the body, mind and soul for healing.

It can be the most work you have ever done in your life. I remember feeling like I was in the fight of my life. My depression felt like it was apart from me and trying to take over me as I fought to overtake it.

Although the symptoms described sound terrible, the grief can somehow be a familiar friend and become the way you connect with a loved one if you are dealing with a death. If you are dealing with the loss of health from a heart attack, you can get attached to the symptoms you are experiencing and be convinced that this is the best it can be and this is now who you are because you don't see any other option. We can be convinced to accept things the way they are because they become familiar. Sometimes the fear of forgetting or the fear of losing who you once were can be so frightening it has you not want to get complete, for fear of losing yourself even more.

Can you think of any examples in your life where this is true for you?

_____

_____

_____

_____

When you go through a divorce you can be more interested in being right about the breakup and the circumstances then getting complete about the relationship. Your resentment about dreams unfulfilled can keep you fuelled and incomplete for a long time and erode your heart. There is something very satisfying about being right when you are going through a loss. It validates us. We gain acceptance from those around us. Being right wards off judgement, knowing that people agree with your side of the story, it keeps us distracted from having to deal with what is really going on underneath. It delays the pain that we might have to confront. There are many, many benefits. So, why wouldn't we seek out the righteousness?

Well, one big reason is that it keeps us in the loss and prevents us from being complete, even though on the other side of being complete is happiness and joy. But we don't see that in the moment. We see the short term benefits and quite frankly, the short term effects are more appealing than seeking long term gain. We want to feel better NOW. Not later!

Can you think of any situations that you are still being RIGHT about?

_____

_____

_____

_____

So, you may start to see some other areas of your life that are not complete having read some of these life situations I am referring to. If that is the case for you. Take a moment and write down where you think you may still be incomplete with a pet dying, a move, a friendship, a divorce, a job, health situation, or whatever else comes to mind.

_____

_____

_____

_____

This may be a good time to go back and review your map. Add the other losses you may not have thought about. It is normal to not identify them the first go around. Take a few minutes and do that now.

So now that you have had a chance to update your map. What were your observations about the map? And, what was it like for you to have to add to the map? There are no correct answers, but this is an exploration and adventure into who you are around grief and it is a good exercise to notice. You could feel discouraged about the fact that there are more incompletions or more losses to deal with. You could feel relieved to have acknowledged them after ignoring them for so long. You could have a light bulb moment having never even realized they were losses for you. Adding these losses may glue some pieces together for you that you had not otherwise seen before and give you some explanation on who you are and why you are the way you are or why you have dealt with things the way you have. Or it could just be an educational exercise and be very matter of fact and you have added them and don't have any thoughts one way or the other.

It is all correct and all good. Just look for yourself.

The Waterfalls

Let's leave our rest stop and carry on through the woods. Probably doesn't feel much like a rest stop doing all this emotional work, but I mean, rest in the sense of stopping to do the work instead of continuing to go full steam ahead and not deal with the emotional work required to get complete.

As we walk through our grief and experience our "good" days and our "bad" days. Sometimes you can go with the flow and handle those bad days by pulling the covers over your head, asking your loved ones for space, or zoning out in front of the TV, or indulging in chocolate, or relaxing with a glass of wine. Or perhaps you go to your bible study group and share about your day, or head to the gym and take it out on the punching bag, or you call a friend and just have a good cry, or bury yourself in good novel. Whatever gets you through those rough days.

REST STOP

Name some of the things you do to get through those "bad" days:

_____

_____

_____

_____

_____

_____

_____

_____

Other times we walk through our journey of grief and we see a bit of a clearing in the forest and we walk towards it. The light is hypnotizing and inviting and yet we take cautious steps not trusting the light completely. The warmth of the light feels soothing as we walk towards it. There is a break in the dense forest and it is so welcoming to have the openness greet us. Our muscles start to relax and our breathing seems calm and get a bit of a skip in our heart beat as we experience the light and warm sunshine in the opening before us. And there in front of us is a beautiful waterfall. Its natural flow, falling down over the rocks as we watch its beauty: forceful and intentional yet effortless. It's mesmerizing to watch. The sounds are thundering as the water smashes down and yet the constant rhythmic sounds are soothing too. The wet smells are refreshing and the feel of the spray on our face is fresh and awakening. All your senses can be activated by this sight.

However, this is not always the case as we walk through our journey of grief. Not that waterfalls aren't sometimes there, but we can experience numbness of some or all of our senses.

What senses are numb for you?

_____

_____

_____

_____

_____

_____

_____

_____

Are there any specific circumstances that you come across that can initiate or trigger this numbness?

_____

_____

_____

_____

Even though we can probably see the beauty of a waterfall on a warm and sunny day, we can also experience the enormous ferocity and danger of a waterfall. Both beautiful and painful experiences can co-exist. It's never black and white when it comes to grief. There is no either/or. There is just all of it.

It's the difference between gazing upon a waterfall, seeing its beauty from a distance, and being in a waterfall, subjected to its forces and unforgiving power.

Here's a quote that really speaks to me about the experience of when you are *really* in the midst of your grief,

"Grief is like a tidal wave that overtakes you, smashes down upon you with unimaginable force, sweeps you up into its darkness where you tumble and crash against unidentifiable surfaces, only to be thrown out on an unknown beach, bruised, reshaped... Grief will make a new person out of you, if it doesn't kill you in the making." – Stephanie Ericsson.

I like this quote because it describes grief so physically. When I reflect on my grief journey, I remember being very surprised at the time, how *physical* grief was. Now looking back on it I also see how transforming it was.

Grief can feel cruel. Like the analogy I just displayed, you can be going along handling your grief moments as they come, using the tools you use to get through those moments, even feeling like there is some light approaching and a glimpse at some "normal life" and then.....BAM! You are tumbling down a fierce waterfall with a force you are not equipped to handle that you didn't even see coming.

Stephanie Ericsson's wave quote speaks to me and my experience of grief. But this may not be your experience. If you have the urge, try to resist making my experience and/or your experience wrong. Remember everyone grieves differently and it all depends on your conversations, experience, circumstances, culture, religion, beliefs, and personality.

REST STOP

Describe your intense feelings of grief. Perhaps it's like being in a dark room all by yourself, falling off a balcony backwards, drowning, or something entirely different. What is it like for you?

_____

_____

_____

_____

_____

A common feeling I have heard from my clients is a part of them died. This is especially true for them when they have lost a loved one, or they have lost their career. We get a big sense of who we are through our relationships and our careers. When one of these leave, sometimes it can lead to the sense of ourselves being gone. This can leave us with feelings of helplessness, being a victim, emptiness, being unfulfilled, and on and on. It can feel like a downward spiral, a domino effect.

The loss of a marriage can have someone question the sacredness of their vows and ultimately their loss of dreams and purpose and their direction in life.

Being sexually violated can lead to a loss of innocence for a child and loss of safety for a grown woman, and then lead to loss of trust and ultimately loss of self-esteem and loss of self.

Having your house robbed or being mugged can be a loss of safety and lead to loss of trust and ultimately loss of your essence and vitality.

Loss of financial status can lead to loss of pride and loss of purpose and fulfillment. I could go on and on with examples that my clients have experienced. The point is, there is never just one loss. A devastating loss will unravel all your unresolved losses and throw them into a messy pile for us to sort out.

REST STOP

List some of the losses that have resulted in other losses for you:

_____

_____

_____

_____

If we have the know-how and the tools outlined in this book, we can tackle our losses in a healthy way and get complete with them as we go so that they don't accumulate as they now do. That is going to require a major shift in how we look at grief. How we treat it ourselves and how we support others while they are grieving. Education is certainly a start and listening to others sharing their stories and their experiences can shed some light on grief, bringing it out in the open, so people are not hidden, and are not awkwardly sidestepping around the conversation leaving people isolated through the process. Bringing grief out into the open is not for the purpose of bringing doom and gloom to the world, but rather brings humanness, light, healing and celebration to the world. Loss is inevitable. Nobody gets out alive, never mind all the losses you experience before your demise.

Take a look at where you "think" you are doing "it" wrong. Or that someone else is doing "it" wrong ("it" being grieving). Just take note and then let that go. Nothing can change if you are making it wrong. If you let it just be how it is, and how it isn't, then it's neutral and you can be involved in moving it to a new place, not "the right" place.

Let's go back and review some of those things you do to get through those bad days. These are our coping strategies. While we are on the topic of not making things wrong, let's not make those coping strategies wrong either. Coping strategies are GOOD. They help us cope. Can you imagine if we didn't have them? It only becomes a problem for us when they become a way of life that prevents us from moving forward and from healing. If people get obsessed with their coping strategies, it could be unhealthy, harmful and even dangerous in some cases. But that is not for you or I to judge. I assume because you are reading this book you have a desire to heal and get complete with your losses, so for that reason, and that reason alone we are going to take a closer look at them. In Pathway Challenge #1 I asked you to name of some your coping skills.

REST STOP

Let's take a minute and review those and make a list of what we do to cope. It can be things we do to get through those "bad days" that we just discussed or it can be something you have acquired as a habit since going through your grief to numb out or cope. Again, don't make them wrong, just bring the awareness to it. Getting honest with yourself through this process will definitely help you in the long run to your healing and getting complete.

_____

_____

_____

_____

_____

_____

What are the circumstances that trigger particular coping strategies?

_____

_____

_____

_____

_____

_____

You may be perfectly content and happy with these coping strategies and be very well aware of what situation or circumstances trigger them and it might be working just fine for you, that's ok. And there may some of you for whom coping strategies might not be working. Or for others, you might get triggered and wish you didn't. The most valuable part of this exercise is to just notice and be aware and be honest with what you are doing to cope. Probably none of your coping strategies are dangerous when used in moderation (obviously I would need to be working with you and be hearing what your coping strategies are, to make a real assessment on this). But if it is legal, then you are probably okay. But being aware and being honest will put you in a place of choice and not in a place of being a victim to them.

One of my clients was watching television obsessively. She hadn't realized before doing this exercise that she was even using this as a coping strategy. She would lose a whole weekend with her butt on the couch and watch decorating shows endlessly. Is this harmful? No, she will probably learn a lot about decorating, very educational. Is she numbing out? Yes, absolutely. Now, doing that every once in a while and being totally aware of it and choosing to plunk your butt on the couch for the weekend and veg in front of the TV, nobody is going to arrest you for it. They might even be envious that they didn't think to do it.

However, once she realized that she was using it to numb out and she was honest about it, she no longer wanted her weekends to be about that. I didn't coach her on the effects of countless hours in front of the television. She saw for herself that she didn't want to numb out anymore. She wanted to get complete with her loss and she did. Does she ever spend the day in front of the television? Probably once in a while, but I can guarantee you she does it by choice and not obsessively every weekend. That's what it looks like to take responsibility for your coping strategies. I had no interest in telling her to stop watching television. It never crossed my mind to do that. She saw that for herself and became part of her healing.

REST STOP

Do you now have any realizations about your coping strategies or things you may be using to numb out that you would like to be honest about?

_____

_____

_____

_____

_____

_____

_____

_____

The Swampy Water

As we leave The Waterfall, and walk along the edge of the river, there are rocks to negotiate and sticks on the ground. We have to be careful where we walk and how we lay our feet depending on the surface. We are making headway along the edge and we see the other side. The forest is behind us and there is this beautiful meadow on the other side. A large gazebo to sit under with trays of fresh fruits, vegetables, pastries and all of your favourite fresh foods to nourish you. There is music playing on the other side and all the beautiful things that appeal to your senses. But, there is swampy water between us and the other side and no bridge. Remember, you can't go over grief, you can't go around it. You must go through it.

Getting from one side of the forest to the meadow requires us to go through some swampy water. It might not be pleasant and you probably don't want to get wet. It's chilly, and there are weeds in the water, and the ground in the swampy water is muddy and difficult to walk in. We will get mud between our toes, and it smells. There are fish in the water and blood suckers. It just isn't pleasant at all. But it is totally necessary to get to the other side.

Nobody ever wants to go into this water. Why would you? It's called Taking Responsibility. It even sounds nasty. The first thing you probably hear is fault and blame. And quite frankly after dealing with all these emotions it is downright exhausting and you might be thinking "Now I have to take the blame and make myself at fault for something? I've just hiked through a forest, dealt with logs on my path, fallen down a waterfall, walked on rocks along the edge of the river. And now you want me to sludge through swampy water? All for this for a beautiful meadow?" The answer is YES, because this meadow represents healing, peace of mind, freedom, and being complete. It is why you are on this journey.

Swamp Secret #1

Let me put your mind at ease. Taking responsibility is NOT blame and it is not placing fault. It looks like the example I gave you about my client and her coping strategy with the TV watching. Mostly it is about BEING HONEST with yourself and you may not be used to looking at things in this way. You have to look at yourself and nobody else. It might sting at first (like dipping into cold water) but, give it some time to sink in, give it a chance, as your muscles relax and you get used to the water, you get more comfortable and you acclimatize, just like you will with taking responsibility. Then it's all about you enjoying the water, just like it's about you enjoying your ride in life and feeling completely alive and fulfilled. Once you allow yourself to be honest it will take the weight off your shoulders that you may or may not even realize you've been carrying around.

❖ ❖ ❖ ❖ ❖ ❖ ❖ ❖ ❖ ❖ ❖ ❖ ❖ ❖ ❖

Swamp Secret #2

When you believe people around you are responsible for the grief you are experiencing, healing is not possible unless all those people take steps towards your healing.

It's crazy to think everyone is going to line up and resolve your broken heart. No, it is up to you and you alone. Now that doesn't mean that others haven't contributed to how you feel.

It just means they are not going to be your solution. <u>You</u> are your solution. Make sense?

❖　❖　❖　❖　❖　❖　❖　❖　❖　❖　❖　❖　❖　❖　❖

REST STOP

What are your thoughts around this so far? Are you prepared to take responsibility?

_____

_____

_____

_____

What are some of your reservations about taking responsibility?

_____

_____

_____

_____

What are you making it mean by taking responsibility?

_____

_____

_____

Is this actually true?

_____

_____

If this you are not yet ready to take responsibility, you need to get this resolved. If you cannot take responsibility for your grief then this will limit your ability to get complete.

Keep in mind that this does not mean you have to take 100% responsibility, but you must be willing to take MOST of the responsibility for your response and reaction to your grief. And know, that whatever is left over, could be limiting you and prevent you from being 100% complete. That's not worth your peace of mind and freedom to be real.

For those who are ready to take responsibility, congratulations. It is a huge step to your healing. It is not only taking responsibility but it is claiming your life as yours. You get to call the shots instead of the circumstances and situations and people in your life calling them for you. True freedom.

Swamp Lesson #1

This is going to be a big piece of work in this process. Normally I would say fasten your seat belts. But since we are out in the woods, strap on your hiking boots and tighten the straps on your backpack.

❖ ❖ ❖ ❖ ❖ ❖ ❖ ❖ ❖ ❖ ❖ ❖ ❖ ❖ ❖

Swamp Lesson #2

This part of the journey will take courage. It is necessary for your healing. You have learned who you are around grief and the beliefs you have and the conversations you have inherited from your family from generations before. You have looked at your history around your grief situations and barriers to your healing and the impacts those barriers have on your day to day vitality and aliveness.

❖ ❖ ❖ ❖ ❖ ❖ ❖ ❖ ❖ ❖ ❖ ❖ ❖ ❖ ❖

Swamp Lesson #3

When you are grieving it can feel very out of control because of the way the emotions come at you from seemingly nowhere. However, when you take responsibility for your response to grief, it will help you feel in control of yourself and your life even when those waves hit.

❖ ❖ ❖ ❖ ❖ ❖ ❖ ❖ ❖ ❖ ❖ ❖ ❖ ❖ ❖

You are probably seeing now that grieving these situations is inevitable but your response to the grief is your choice and you can now take responsibility for your response to grief. How you do your grief is up to you.

Taking responsibility would look like you getting complete with the grief that is stopping you from living your life to the fullest. It might have been your grief situation that had you purchase this curriculum. Sometimes (most times) by going through this journey you reveal a grief situation to be resolved that you didn't realize was stopping or impacting you in your life. We are going to move into that process now.

The Meadow

Now that you have taken responsibility you probably feel like you are more in the driver's seat than before. This is the feeling of empowerment. You can now come from a place in your heart called choice. You are choosing to get complete and heal from the pain of your grief. Keep the vision of the meadow in your mind. I started to create a vision of a pleasant meadow as a representation of joy, peace of mind. Create it in your mind for what appeals to your senses. The picture, the food, the music, perhaps there is artwork on easels, or dancing or yoga mats, or paints, healing stones, friends laughing or children playing. Whatever warms your heart, makes your heart sing or invokes feelings of love and joy. That is where we are going. It is in our reach. The forest, logs, waterfalls and swampy waters are all behind us. We are equipped and using all the tools from our backpack.

Meadow Challenge

Describe your meadow:

_____

_____

_____

_____

_____

_____

Choose a relationship or situation to get complete with.

_____

_____

_____

What made you choose this relationship or situation to get complete with?

_____

_____

_____

_____

What do you think is possible and what would you like to be possible if you were to get complete?

_____

_____

_____

_____

What do you see about this relationship/situation from what you have learned about yourself (i.e. how you are with grief, your beliefs and coping strategies)?

_____

_____

_____

_____

_____

_____

Review your grief situation and look for ways that you can take responsibility for your response to the grief.

_____

_____

_____

What part of the situation are you responsible for?

_____

_____

_____

What response can you take responsibility for?

_____

_____

_____

Where could you have chosen a different response? What is the new response you could have chosen?

_____

_____

_____

❖ ❖ ❖ ❖ ❖ ❖ ❖ ❖ ❖ ❖ ❖ ❖ ❖ ❖ ❖

Great work! Now you can take steps to get complete with your grief.

Amends, Forgiveness and Freedom

These three elements are the keys to you getting complete and being free of the pain that you are carrying in your heart.

Amends. To say sorry is to have a feeling or expressing sympathy, pity, or regret

Forgiveness. Forgiveness is the process of ceasing to feel resentment, indignation or anger against another person for a perceived offense, difference or mistake, or ceasing to demand punishment or restitution.

Freedom. This is the state of being free or at liberty rather than in confinement or under physical restraint

Draw a line in the sand right now, right here

Meadow Exercise #3

What are you willing to make amends for?

_____

_____

_____

_____

What are you willing to forgive them/yourself for?

_____

_____

_____

_____

What are you willing to have freedom around?

_____

_____

_____

_____

❖ ❖ ❖ ❖ ❖ ❖ ❖ ❖ ❖ ❖ ❖ ❖ ❖ ❖ ❖

You will really want to embrace this next part of the pathway. It is essential to your healing and getting complete. It is the most beautiful part of the forest. You will start to see the sun shining through the trees, and feel the warmth of the sunshine on your face. You will be aware of the breeze in the air, and feel it in your hair and on your face and your whole body. Your senses will awaken like never before. You will notice the intricate shapes of the leaves and how the breeze moves them on their branches. How they sway but are steadfast. You will be aware of all the beauty around you and you will be connected to all that beauty as you realize you are a part of it.

Forgiveness Secret #1

Forgiveness does not mean you are condoning the behaviour or that you are agreeing to any wrong doing. You are not justifying or explaining or making allowances for, or compensating for. Forgiveness doesn't excuse their behaviour Forgiveness prevents their behaviour from destroying your heart.

❖ ❖ ❖ ❖ ❖ ❖ ❖ ❖ ❖ ❖ ❖ ❖ ❖ ❖ ❖

Forgiveness Secret #2

Forgiveness is a gift for you, not them. It is to set your heart free of carrying the anger or resentment towards the person or circumstance. It is to set you free, not them. Carrying around resentment about someone or something is like letting them/it live rent free in your head. It is only hurting you.

❖ ❖ ❖ ❖ ❖ ❖ ❖ ❖ ❖ ❖ ❖ ❖ ❖ ❖ ❖

Forgiveness Secret #3

*There is **no benefit** to sharing this part with the other person. It is very important to understand that this is really about you and not them. They do not need to hear your work on forgiveness. It could actually backfire on you and open up old wounds and you could get yourself re-traumatized by this person. It is not an exercise you do with the person you are forgiving. This might seem strange at first but think about it, it's not like you are going to them and saying "You're off the hook, and I forgive you" and they feel better. They may not even have felt bad in the first place. That's why it's about YOU. It's you carrying this around, not them. They do not even have to know that you are forgiving them. If/when you forgive them and you get complete then you get to choose how you go forward with that person (or not) and if you choose to go forward with this person, then your actions and behaviour and way of "being" will demonstrate forgiveness. Down the road if you want to discuss forgiveness, if it feels safe, then broach the subject. But until then, this is your work, and only yours.*

Freedom

When you are willing to let something go it will create an opening for freedom to be present in your life. Something will shift, either a way of looking at things, or your reaction to something or feeling you get. It can look different for everyone, but one thing is for certain, something has shifted and you will like it.

Freedom Secret #1

Freedom does mean letting go but it does not mean you forget, it just means you are letting go of the pain associated with it.

❖ ❖ ❖ ❖ ❖ ❖ ❖ ❖ ❖ ❖ ❖ ❖ ❖ ❖ ❖

Freedom Secret #2

Just because you let go, doesn't mean that a circumstance won't arise where you might get "hooked" again and you have to let go again. Don't beat yourself up thinking "I already did this work." Sometimes these feelings or thoughts can be deep rooted. Be grateful you did the work and recognize it is just that "thing" coming up again and be grateful you have the knowledge and tools to let it go. You will notice it comes up less and less and you will notice you can let go faster and faster and eventually you won't get "hooked" anymore.

❖ ❖ ❖ ❖ ❖ ❖ ❖ ❖ ❖ ❖ ❖ ❖ ❖ ❖ ❖

Freedom Secret #3

Don't believe everything you see. It might seem like an "out there" concept but we really do create our own reality. Believing everything around us is a pitfall and prevents us from finding our freedom. Nothing is as it seems. Everyone has their own story that they keep close. When you are suffering, it always seems like everyone else out there is thriving and happy. We just all get good at covering up and carrying on. Just like you have been doing. It takes courage to stop and really deal with what's going on. Sometimes it seems scary to get off the "Life is ok" train and go to a darker, sadder place to heal, but it is a courageous and worthwhile journey and the access to your heart and freedom. Grief is painful, but it is only a resting place and not a destination. So don't believe everything you see.

❖ ❖ ❖ ❖ ❖ ❖ ❖ ❖ ❖ ❖ ❖ ❖ ❖ ❖ ❖

Freedom Secret #4

Trust that exactly where you are in your healing is where you are supposed to be, nowhere else. There is always a reason we go through the things we do. There are always lessons and insights to receive in these times of grief. The lessons will vary but it will always be connected to love.

❖ ❖ ❖ ❖ ❖ ❖ ❖ ❖ ❖ ❖ ❖ ❖ ❖ ❖ ❖

Speaking about love, let's explore a bit about love. I find it such a difficult thing to explain. But I know for me, I had to be in a dark place before I saw the light and for me that light was love. All this work and exploration you are doing is to bring you to a place of love. When you tap into that love, something shifts. You can't explain it, it has to be felt. That is what true freedom feels like… Love, Love, Love. And love will look and feel differently for everyone. Miracles start to happen when you feel love. Things that would not normally happen, happen. Relationships that were not thriving before, thrive. Feelings that were not there before, become present. You just have to experience it for yourself.

Although love is internal and eternal, love can be accessed through events and people and circumstances that occur every day. Love shows up in so many different ways. A neighbour can show up in your life in a special way that you couldn't have predicted, your brother who you haven't spoken to in years suddenly is back in your life, you meet people through these grief circumstances that you would not have otherwise met, like a parent of your child you hadn't met before and you are so grateful for the friendship you can't even imagine them not in your life. You might learn a new skill like painting when you thought you couldn't paint a straight line, yet you are suddenly creating beautiful works of art. You might start writing poetry when you couldn't rhyme a single word to another before. You might suddenly enjoy baking cakes and you wouldn't have given it the time of day before. You might take a dance class with your two left feet or sign up for a course in photography that you always wanted to take. You might take an interest in your garden and it brings out your creative side. You might take up the piano or guitar and find solace in the music you make. You might suddenly take an interest in your car care like never before and start adding accessories and create a new pride in your vehicle, or buy a telescope and get interested in constellations and comets. Or you might start appreciating bubble baths and start adding candles to enjoy the experience even more. You might take up mediation or yoga and you thought it was for those Zen-like people before. Maybe you start volunteering at the local soup kitchen or start attending your community church or you might sponsor a child in a developing country. Maybe you find a board you want to sit on to support a cause that speaks to your heart or you volunteer at your local hospital. And, on and on. This is such a limited list of possibilities. It is difficult to see this when you are still in the dark place but trust me, it will happen. That's right, love will just happen if you welcome it in and it might show up in unexpected places, so keep your eyes and ears open to receive it.

Freedom Secret #5

Miracles happen every day, we just have to stop to notice.

❖ ❖ ❖ ❖ ❖ ❖ ❖ ❖ ❖ ❖ ❖ ❖ ❖ ❖ ❖

Okay, let's get back to work. You have chosen the area, or relationship you want to get complete with. You can see that this is the loss that is holding you back from being completely fulfilled in life. The loss that is blocking your heart from being completely open and having access to all the love you know you want to feel in your heart and have it translated into your life.

After doing all this exploration on grief and loss and looking at who you are with grief and your coping strategies, your distractions, your beliefs. You have probably dug up a lot of old, otherwise buried and unsettled emotions. You could be feeling like emotions are bubbling up. You could be feeling overwhelmed and you could feel like you want to stop. You have learned a lot about yourself and it could feel like you

76

have learned what you need to learn and you just want to get on with life and not do any more work. Remember what I talked about earlier about it being the same distance back as it is forward. Don't stop now. Don't stop before the miracle. Remember the meadow you created.

On the other hand, you could be excited about your exploration and see the end in sight. You could be relieved that you are about to get complete and be excited about what is in store for you. You might be starting to realize that when you saw yourself shattered into small pieces of glass and your attempts to put it all back into that form that you once knew, is now not an option and you may be realizing that this is not the point. There is no putting back all the shattered pieces to be the same as it had been. There is only the opportunity to heal and become the healed person you are meant to be. You are choosing to allow grief to change you and not allowing yourself to stay the same place where you are. You have realized the journey must be taken alone. Not by yourself because there are people and resources to support you in your journey, but ultimately this is your journey and yours alone.

By now you may have discovered that the dark tunnel you have been walking in does have a light (and it's not the headlight of a train ☺) it's the light of love waiting for you to walk towards it. You realize that growth only comes from our deepest pain and you are leaning into it instead of resisting it or fighting it. You are probably noticing that you are more aware of living in the moment. This may have come out of necessity because when we are in our darkest most painful experiences, it is all we are capable of. I remember someone saying to me, it is a miracle that from moment to moment you are able to have your lungs move in and out from moment to moment and this was so very true for me. It really puts "slowing down" into perspective when you think of your life moments in terms of literally one breath at a time and literally putting one foot in front of the other to take a single step. Once you have experienced life broken down in these moments of NOW, you will always know this experience that others who have not experienced this deep intense grief may not have experienced and it is not something you can explain. You will just know what I am talking about and at some point you will cherish it.

This is one of the gifts I received and I hope you can at some point look back and realize this as a gift too. This is one of the reasons that I see Grief connects people in a deep intimate way. It was in my rawest state that I felt the most real. I was both undeniably devastated and in my deepest agony and yet there was a sense of elation as well. It's those experiences that you cannot explain, you just have to experience them. When people have experienced this, it unifies them in ways they cannot explain.

REST STOP

How have you allowed Grief to change you?

_____

_____

_____

What do you now see as possible if you continue to allow Grief to change you?

_____

_____

_____

What gifts have you received from your journey of grief and loss?

_____

_____

_____

_____

Do you have any apprehensions on taking the next steps? If so, what are they?

_____

_____

_____

_____

Are you willing to move forward despite your apprehensions?

_____

_____

_____

_____

What did you have to overcome for yourself to move forward?

_____

_____

_____

_____

The Compass

We are going to write a letter to get complete with the loss you have chosen. This letter must contain critical elements and you must be willing to be perfectly honest and you must be willing to take responsibility for your response to your grief. This letter (Compass) is going to lead you to the end of the path and lead you to getting complete.

There are a few elements to this letter.

Compass Exercise #1

First you must look at the relationship you are getting complete with and identify anything you want to say sorry about. This is the part where you get to take responsibility.

List some things you are sorry about in the relationship:

I am sorry _____

I am sorry _____

I am sorry_____

I am sorry _____

❖ ❖ ❖ ❖ ❖ ❖ ❖ ❖ ❖ ❖ ❖ ❖ ❖ ❖ ❖

Compass Exercise #2

Now look at where you can forgive the person/situation you are getting complete with:

I forgive you for _____

I forgive you for _____

I forgive you for _____

I forgive you for _____

❖ ❖ ❖ ❖ ❖ ❖ ❖ ❖ ❖ ❖ ❖ ❖ ❖ ❖ ❖

Compass Exercise #3

Now look for things that you wish you could have said. This is all unspoken communication that if they were here and you had another chance to speak to them or speak about the situation, this is what you would say:

I wish I could have told you _____

I wish I could have said _____

I wish I would have _____

I wish there was more time for us to _____

I wish we went _____

I wish things were _____

I wish _____

I wish _____

I wish _____

Make sure you say EVERYTHING you want to say in this section. Nothing left unsaid. Just keep writing until you can't think of anything else to say. These are just prompters. You word it however you want to that fits your situation.

❖ ❖ ❖ ❖ ❖ ❖ ❖ ❖ ❖ ❖ ❖ ❖ ❖ ❖ ❖

Compass Exercise #4

Now if you are ready, let's take this to paper. Write your letter and let your person know you have been looking at your grief and your life and you need to get complete with them. (Say this in your letter). Then write your apologies, forgiveness and all your unspoken communication. Get it all said on paper. There is no right or wrong way to do this, but there are more effective ways. Make sure you are honest. It's most effective if you keep the focus on you and not them. If you need to write ten pages to get it all out, then do it. If you can summarize it in one page then do it. This might prompt tears and that is okay, and you may not shed a tear, and that's okay too. Don't put any expectations on yourself. Remember you are exactly where you need to be. All your reactions are dependent on you and your life experiences and your relationship, your previous grief work, your personality, and so much more.

❖ ❖ ❖ ❖ ❖ ❖ ❖ ❖ ❖ ❖ ❖ ❖ ❖ ❖ ❖

Compass Exercise #5

Once you write the letter, then read it aloud six times. When you read it, I want you to take your time and FEEL the words. See if there is any "charge" in any of the apologies or any of the forgiveness statements. Does it still pull at your heart? Do you still feel some withheld resentment? If so, then you may not be complete. There might be something you are still being right about or holding onto and not willing to forgive.

❖ ❖ ❖ ❖ ❖ ❖ ❖ ❖ ❖ ❖ ❖ ❖ ❖ ❖ ❖

Compass Exercise #6

If you know what it is, go back and do more work round those areas. Go back to that section of the workbook and ask yourself the questions again and dig deeper. When you get to them, then read the letter again and see if it feels different.

Ultimately there should be no "charge" after reading your letter six times. Being complete reveals itself as a neutral essence. Not that you don't have feelings but, there is no "charge" to it, no energy surrounding the statements. You need to be in touch with your heart to sense this.

"It's your Heart that knows the path. The mind is just there to organize the steps." ~ Jeff Brown

❖ ❖ ❖ ❖ ❖ ❖ ❖ ❖ ❖ ❖ ❖ ❖ ❖ ❖ ❖

Compass Bonus

If you are not sure and want to have some guidance and reassurance on this to ensure you are complete, since you have done so much work to get here – I do not want anyone to walk away feeling defeated or unsatisfied from doing this work – you can arrange a half hour Completion Call with me. I am committed to everyone who has taken the time to do this work, and I am passionate about people getting complete and being free from the burdens of unresolved grief and loss. My gift to you for purchasing this workbook and doing the work is a half hour Completion Call with me at a reduced rate. You can read your letter to me and I will let you know if I believe you are complete from your letter. If you are not complete I can tell you what areas I think you need to do more work on.

Simply email me at <u>cheryllynneparker@gmail.com</u> and we can arrange a date and time for a call together. Please put "Completion Call Request" in the email subject line so that I get back to you as soon as possible.

❖ ❖ ❖ ❖ ❖ ❖ ❖ ❖ ❖ ❖ ❖ ❖ ❖ ❖ ❖

If you are complete and you know you are complete...... Congratulations!!!! You probably feel a shift in your heart. A lightness or relief. It's an Ahhhhhhhhhhhhhh moment. You have done a great job exploring and getting to the root of your grief. You will be grateful for doing this work. Your spirit will feel lifted and everything will feel more vital in your life. It will open your heart to love like it could not before. You might see people in a different light, you might notice things that you didn't notice before, colours might seem brighter, stars might seem more defined, traffic lighter, it could show up in any number of different ways, but there is definitely a shift. You will probably feel more connected to people that you have close relationship with. Grief purifies us and unifies us. Brings out a realness in us that is beautiful and authentic. You no longer need or will want to carry the burden of this loss. You are free.

As you look back at the forest you have just walked through, we can now see the huge tree that had fallen in our path. The tree is dead. We can now look at that big gaping hole in the ground with the exposed soil, and we can see ferns growing and wild flowers popping up between the ferns. The hole is now full of water and the forest animals come to drink from the pond that has been created. We couldn't stop the tree from dying when we came upon it but, we can see the beauty that gets created from the destruction it once caused. One could take the analogy as time healing, but don't be fooled. Even

84

with nature's miracles, there is so much going on to have that tree die and have the ferns and flowers grow and the water to be provided for the forest wild life. Yes, time is an element but, nature was at work the whole time to create that beauty. The tree did not fall one day to have ferns and flowers growing immediately the day after. There was a process. Congratulations and thank you for allowing me to guide you through your process. Go forth and create your beauty.

Wishing you love and light on your future paths.

Cheryl